It's Easy To Play The Corrs.

Wise Publications
London / New York / Paris / Sydney / Copenhagen / Madrid

Exclusive Distributors:

Music Sales Limited
8/9 Frith Street, London W1V 5TZ, England.

Music Sales Pty Limited
120 Rothschild Avenue, Rosebery, NSW 2018, Australia.

Order No. AM958815
ISBN 0-7119-7376-8

www.internetmusicshop.com

Book design by Michael Bell Design.
Cover photograph courtesy of All Action.
Compiled by Peter Evans.
Music arranged by Stephen Duro.
Music processed by Allegro Reproductions.

Printed in the United Kingdom by
Caligraving Limited, Thetford, Norfolk.

Dreams

Words & Music by Stevie Nicks

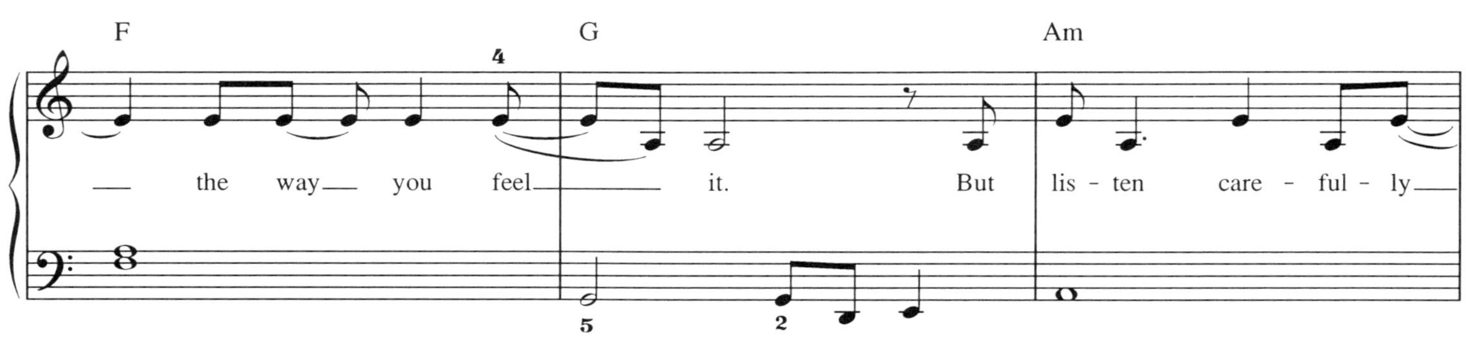

Dm7
F
G
to the sound of your lone - li - ness, like a
F
G
Fmaj7
heart - beat drives you mad in the still - ness of re - mem -
G
F
G
- ber - ing what you had, and what you lost,
F
G
F
and what you had,
G
F
G
and what you lost,
Yeah,

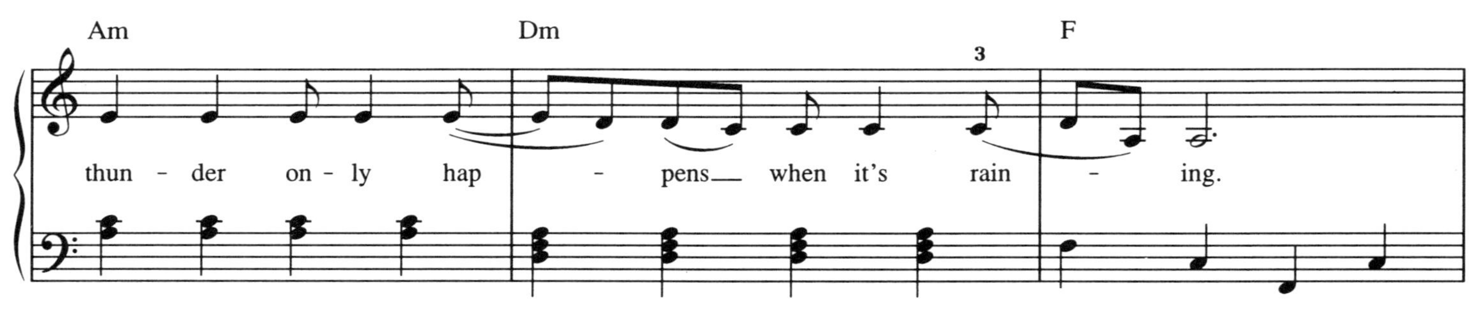
Am
Dm
F
3
thun - der on - ly hap - pens when it's rain - ing.

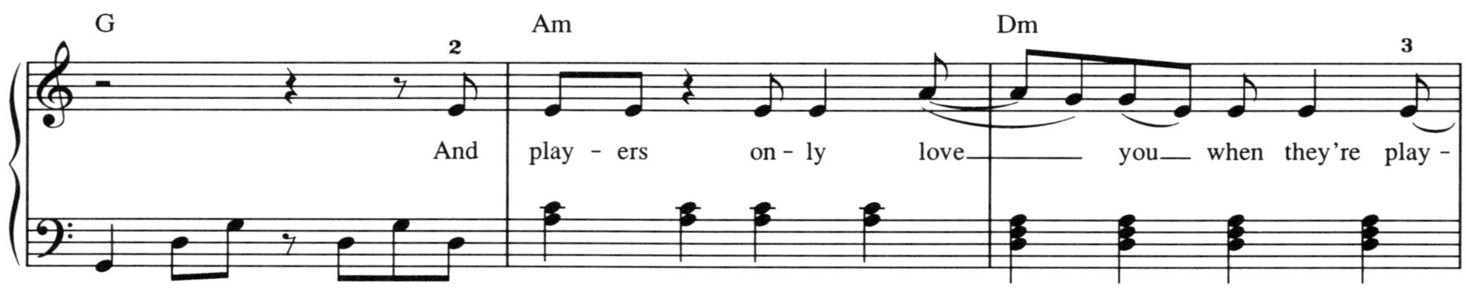
G
Am
Dm
2
3
And play - ers on - ly love you when they're play -

F
G
Am
- ing.
Yeah, wo - men they will come

Dm
F
G
4
and they will go.

Am
Dm
F
When the rain wash - es you clean you'll know.

Verse 2:

Now here I go again I see the crystal vision
But I keep my visions to myself
Well it's only me who wants to wrap around your dreams
And have you any dreams you'd like to sell?
Dreams of loneliness.

Like a heartbeat *etc.*

Forgiven, Not Forgotten

Words & Music by Andrea Corr, Caroline Corr, Sharon Corr & Jim Corr

G Dm F
and heard her whis - per of a name long for - giv -
G Am C G
- en but not for - got - ten. You're for -
Dm G Am
- giv - en not for - got - ten, you're for - giv - en not for -
G Dm
- got - ten, you're for - giv - en not for -
G Am C G
- got - ten, you're not for - got - ten.

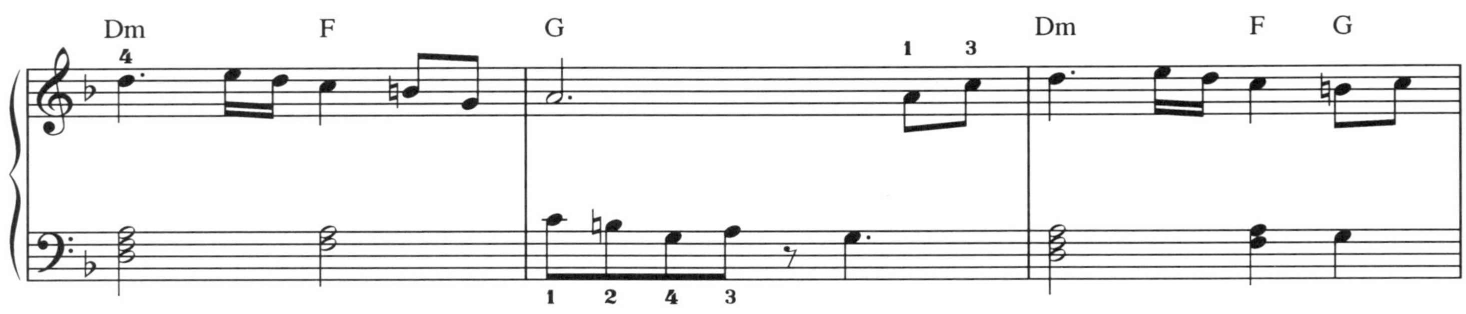
Dm F G Dm F G
4
1 3
1 2 4 3

Em Dm F G Dm F G
4
2 4

Em Dm G
Still a - lone,
star - ing on,

Dm G Dm
wish - ing her life good - bye.
As she goes
search - ing for a man long for - giv -

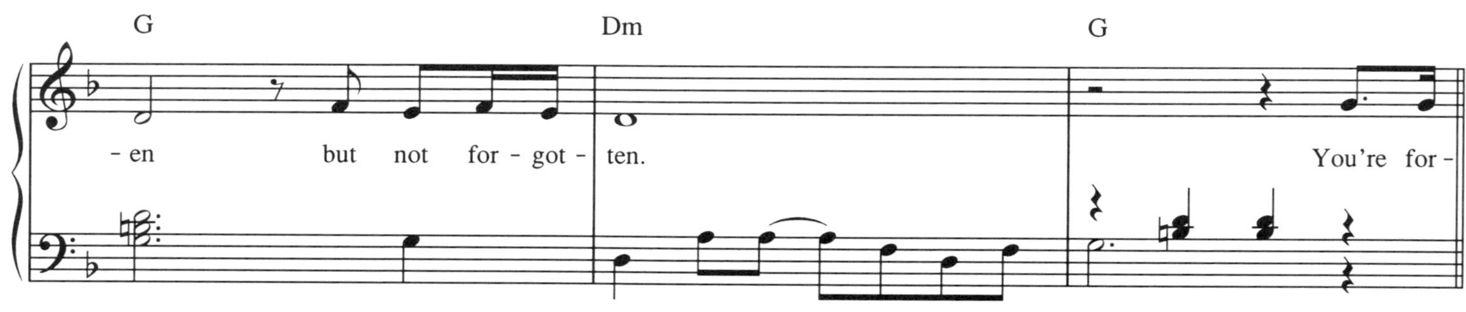
G Dm G
- en but not for - got - ten.
You're for -

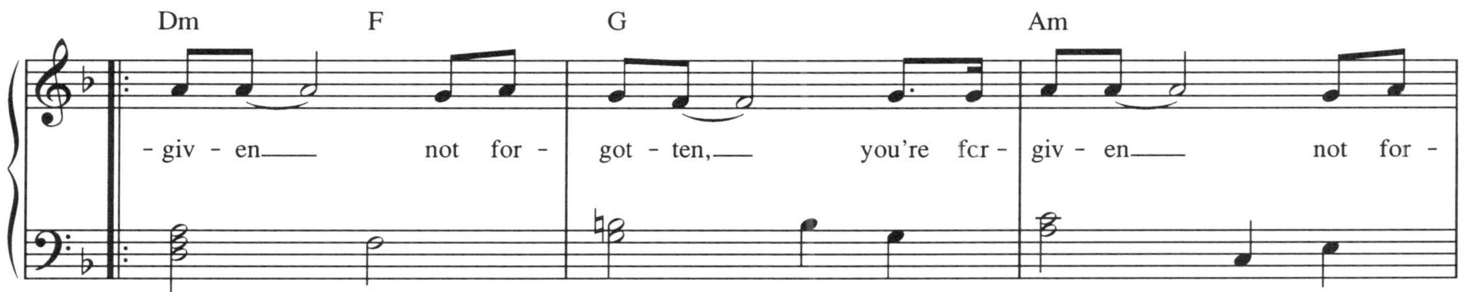

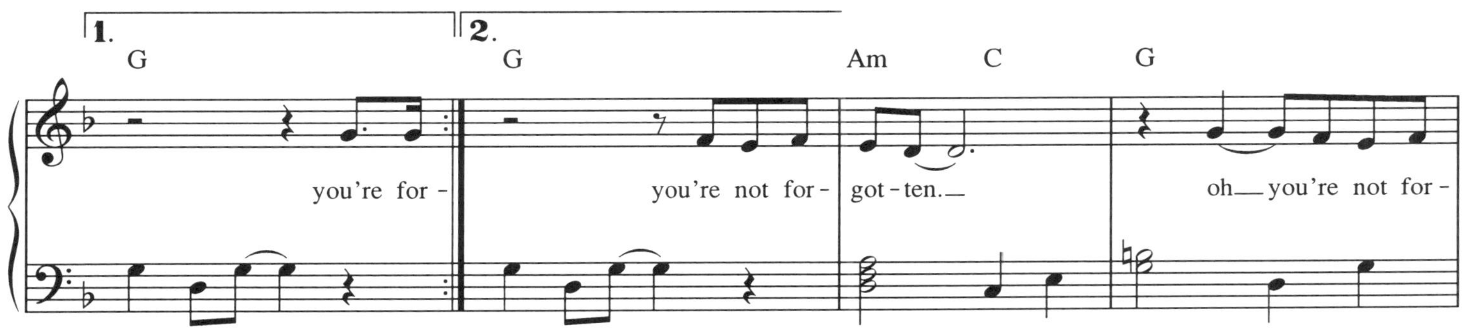

Verse 2:

A bleeding heart torn apart, left on an icy bed
In a room where they once lay face to face
Nothing could get in the way
But now the memories of a man are haunting her day
And the craving never fades
She's still dreaming of a man long forgiven, but not forgotten...

Hopelessly Addicted

Words & Music by Andrea Corr, Caroline Corr,
Sharon Corr, Jim Corr & Oliver Leiber

Em7
Asus4
A
words, I would swear it was a lie. I don't know
D G Bm A D G
why but sud - den - ly I'm fall - ing,
Bm A Bm G Bm7 Cmaj7
Was I so
I was
blind, I was
Em D G
To Coda
lov - ing you all the time. Now I'm hope - less - ly ad -
1.
D
- dict - ed, help - less - ly at - tract - ed.

Em C
2.
2. I'll make a
- dict - ed, na - tural - ly we act - ed.
F♯m G C G D F♯m
G C Asus4 A
D.S. al Coda
I don't know
CODA
D G Bm A D G
- ict - ed, help - less - ly at - tract - ed,
Bm7 A Bm7 G Bm7 C
che - mic - ally re - act - ed, I was

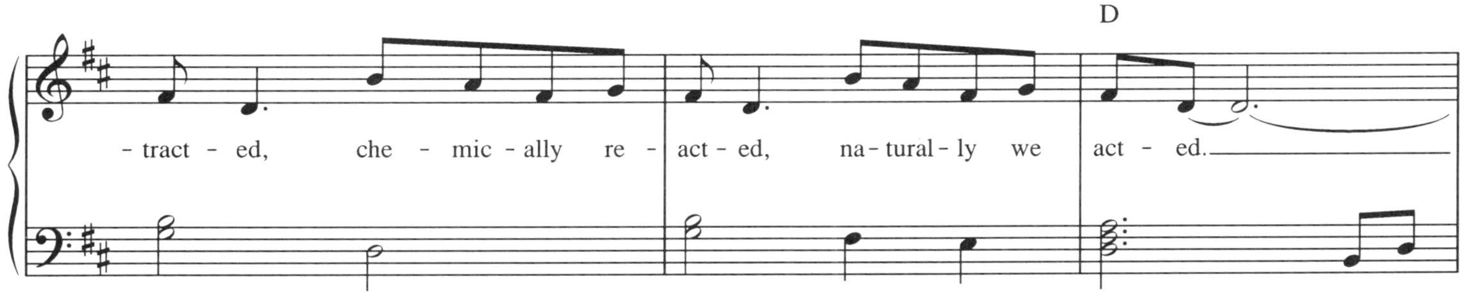

Verse 2:

I'll make a wish this day
And I'll send it to the heavens
That we will always stay
Entwined like this forever.

And though the world may change
'Cause nothing stays the same
I know we will survive.

I don't know why *etc.*

Don't Say You Love Me

Words & Music by Andrea Corr, Caroline Corr,
Sharon Corr, Jim Corr & Carole Bayer Sager

F/C G/C Csus4 C F/C G/C
-less for ev - er, don't tell me you need me if you're not gon - na stay, don't
Dm7 C F G F C
give me this feel - ing, I'll on - ly be - lieve it, make it
D.C. al Coda
Dm7 F/G G C F G
real or take it all a - way.
CODA
G C Csus4 C F/C G/C
choice. Don't say you love me un - less for - ev - er, don't
Csus4 C F/C G/C Dm7 C
tell me you need me if you're not gon - na stay, don't give me this feel - ing, I'll

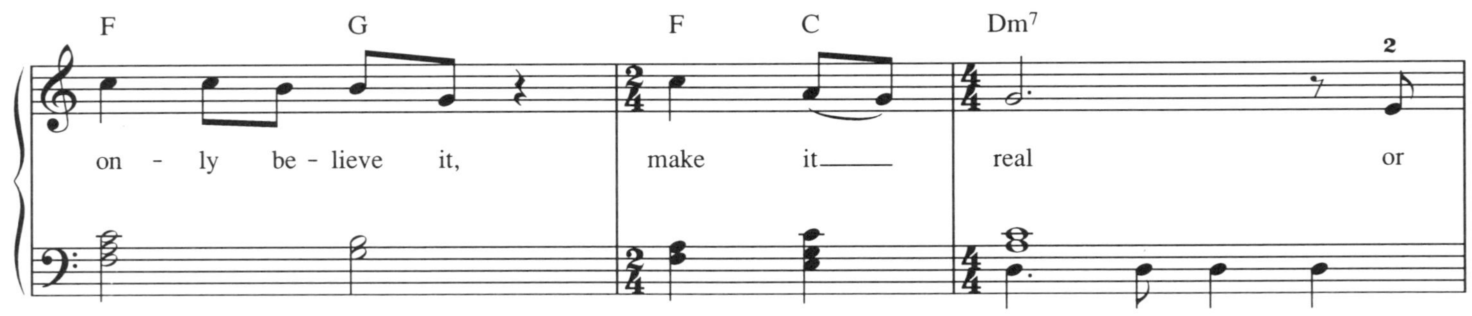
F
G
F
C
Dm7
2
on - ly be - lieve it,
make it
real
or
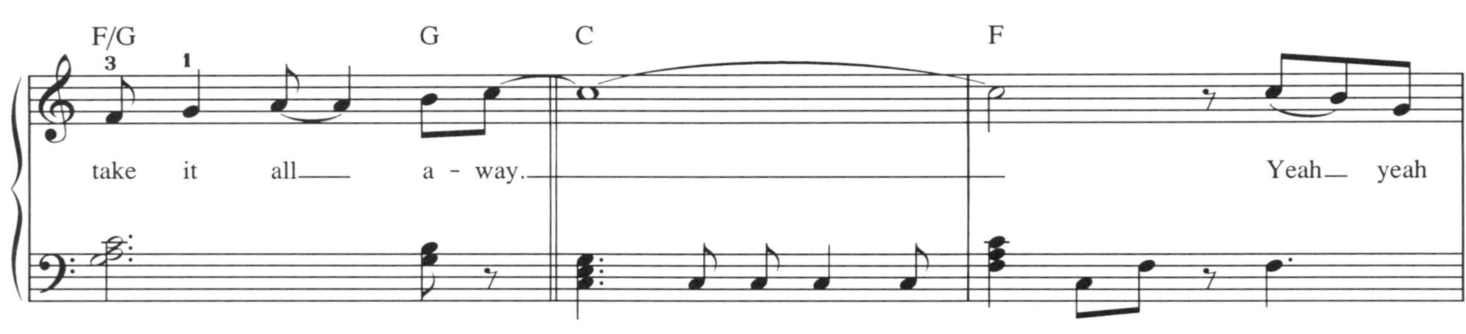
F/G
G
C
F
3
1
take it all a - way.
Yeah yeah
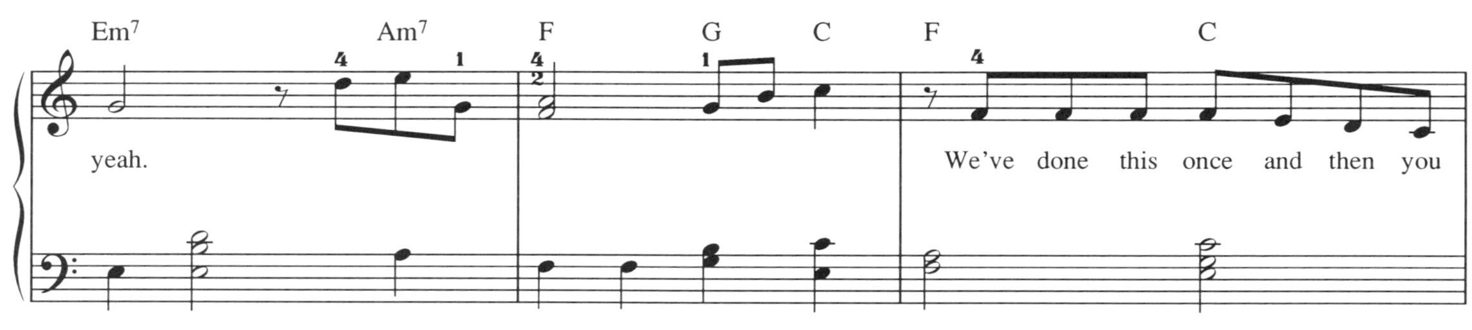
Em7
Am7
F
G
C
F
C
4
1
4
2
1
4
yeah.
We've done this once and then you

Dm7
C
F
C
Dm7
F/G
G
3
1
closed the door,
don't let me fall a - gain for
noth - ing more, don't

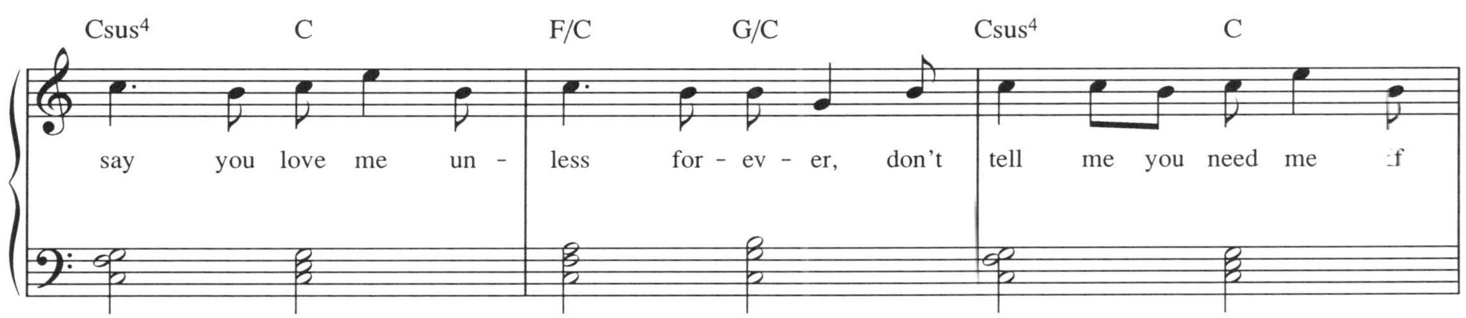
Csus4
C
F/C
G/C
Csus4
C
say you love me un - less for - ev - er, don't tell me you need me if

F/C
G/C
Dm7
C
F
G
you're not gon - na stay, don't give me this feel - ing, I'll on - ly be - lieve it,

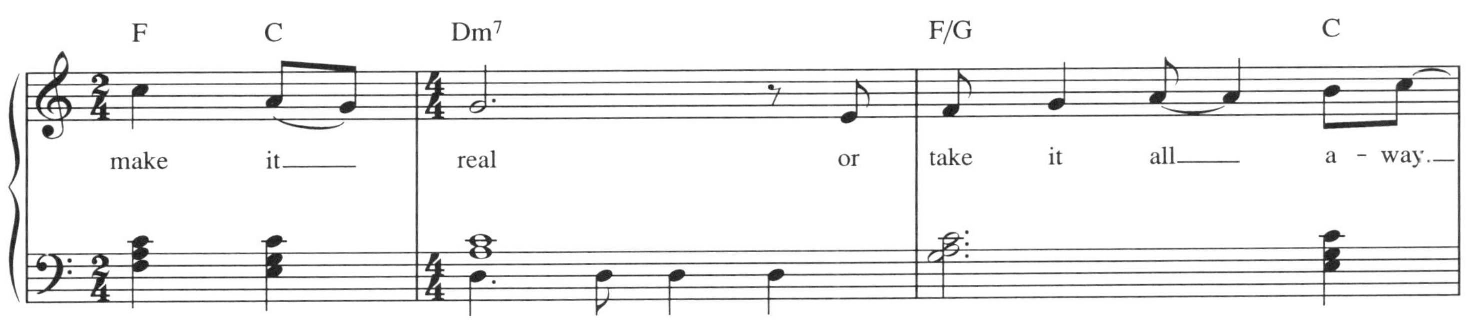
F
C
Dm7
F/G
C
make it real or take it all a - way.

F
C
Dm7
G
Csus4
C
Don't tell me you need me if

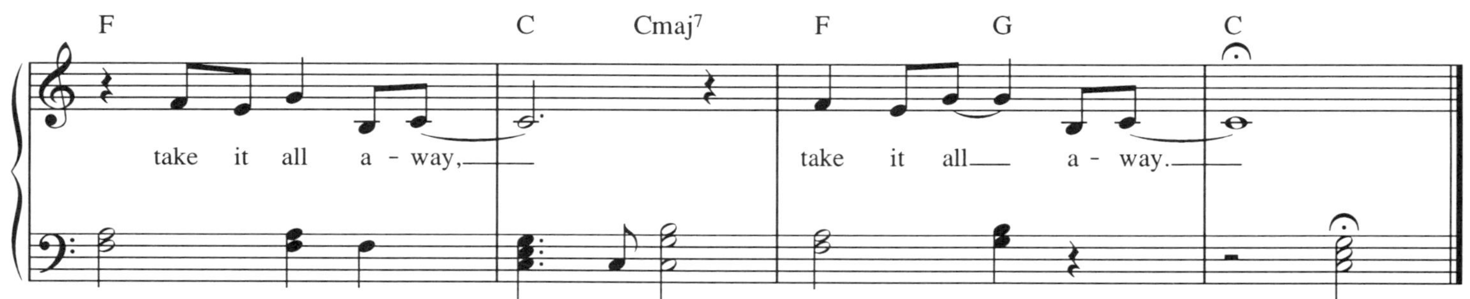

Verse 2:

I know this face I'm wearing now
I've seen this in my eyes
And though it feels so great I'm still afraid
That you'll be leaving anytime.

Verse 3:

I've caught myself smiling alone
Just thinking of your voice,
And dreaming of your touch it's all too much
You know I don't have any choice.

Love Gives Love Takes

Words & Music by Andrea Corr, Sean Hosein, Dane de Viller,
Stacey Piersa, Elliot Wolff & Oliver Leiber

Second time only
Fm6
F
Am
G
C
e - mo - tion.
Love breaks and love di - vides,
love laughs and love can make you cry.
I can't be - lieve
the ways that
1.
Dm7
N.C.
love can give and love can take a - way.
Fadd9
Gadd9
2.
love can give and love can take a - way.

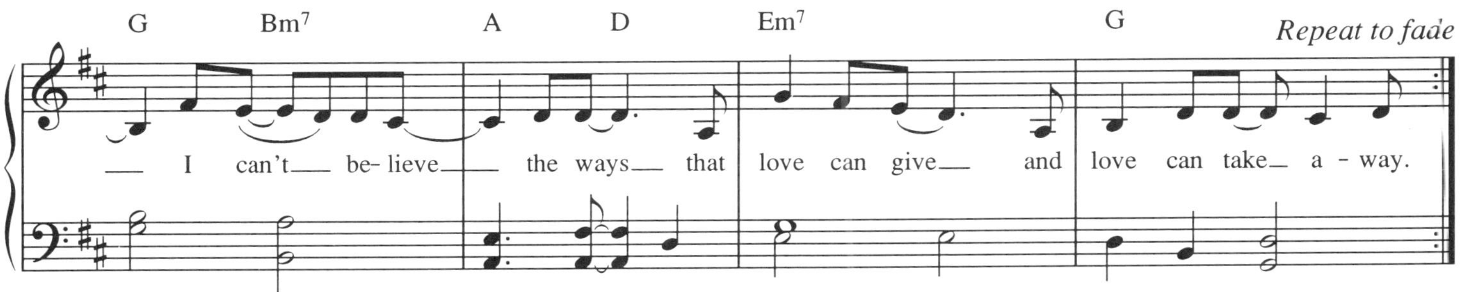

Verse 2:

I find it hard to explain
It's crazy but it's happening,
And I'm falling again
Much further than I've ever been.
I'm falling deeper than the ocean
I am lost in this emotion.

Love breaks and love divides *etc.*

No Good For Me

Words & Music by Andrea Corr, Caroline Corr, Sharon Corr & Jim Corr

E♭maj7 F Gm F E♭maj7 F
no, no good for me, you have no i - dea
Cm Gm E♭maj7 B♭
that I'm walk - ing through the clouds when you're look - ing at me, I'm feel - ing like a
Gm E♭maj7 B♭ Gm
child vul - n'ra - bi - li - ty I am shak - ing like a leaf if you move be - side me
E♭maj7 B♭ Gm 1. F Gm
and you're all that I see, but it's no good for me.
2. F Gm E♭maj7 B♭
no it's no good for me, no good for me.

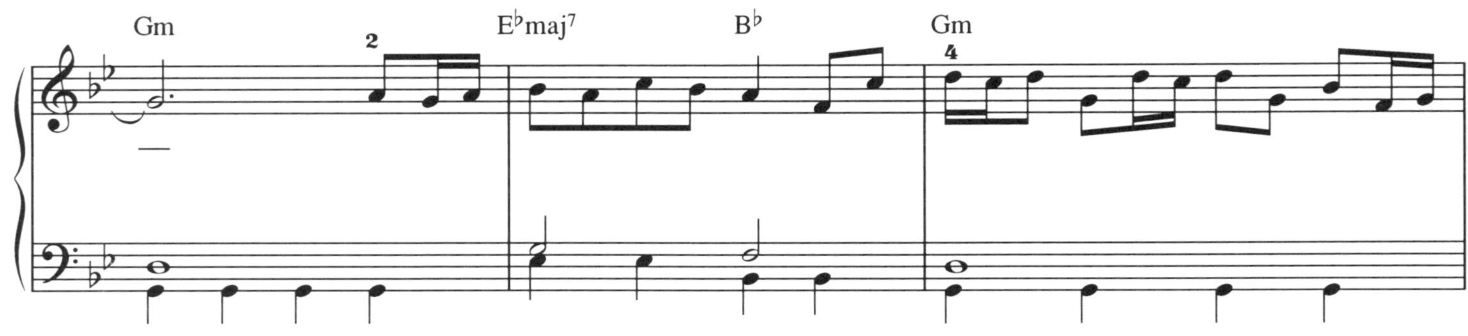
Gm
2
E♭maj7
B♭
Gm
4

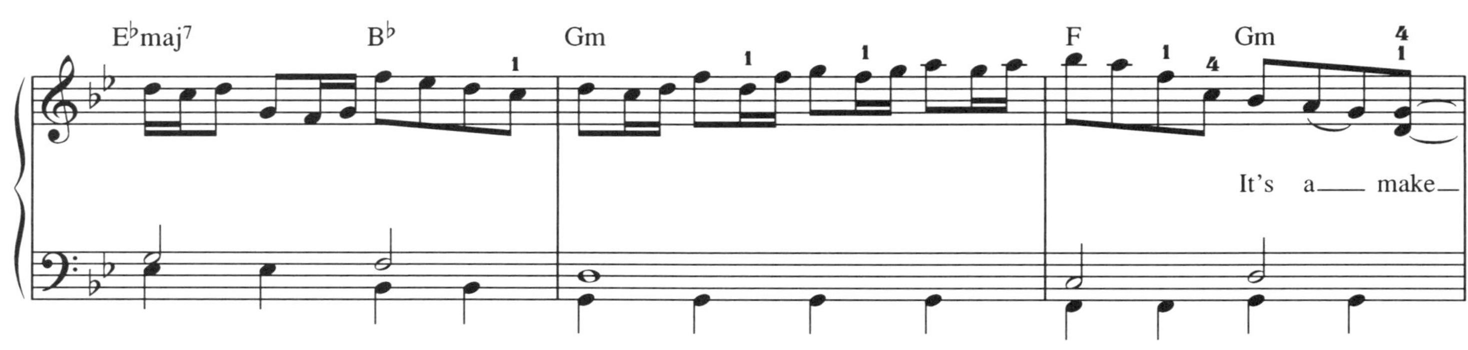
E♭maj7
B♭
1
Gm
1
1
F
1
4
Gm
4
1
It's a make

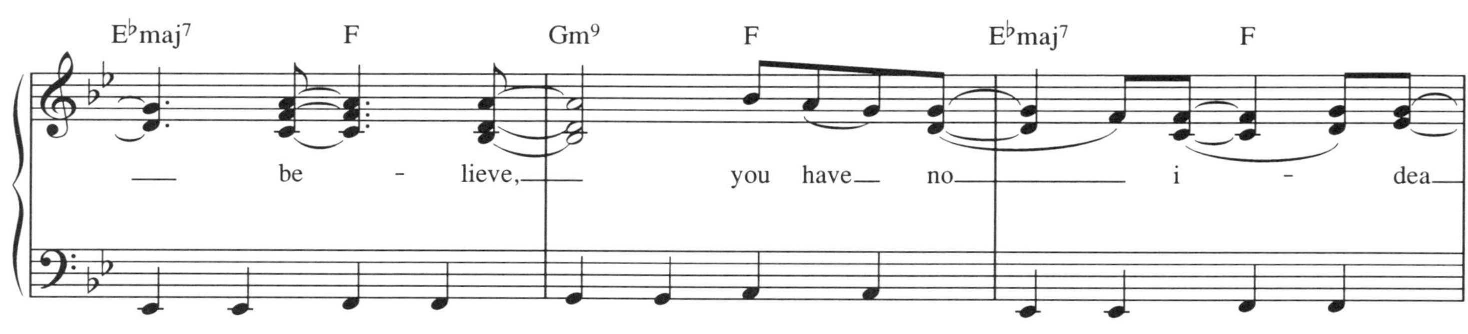
E♭maj7
F
Gm9
F
E♭maj7
F
be - lieve,
you have no
i - dea

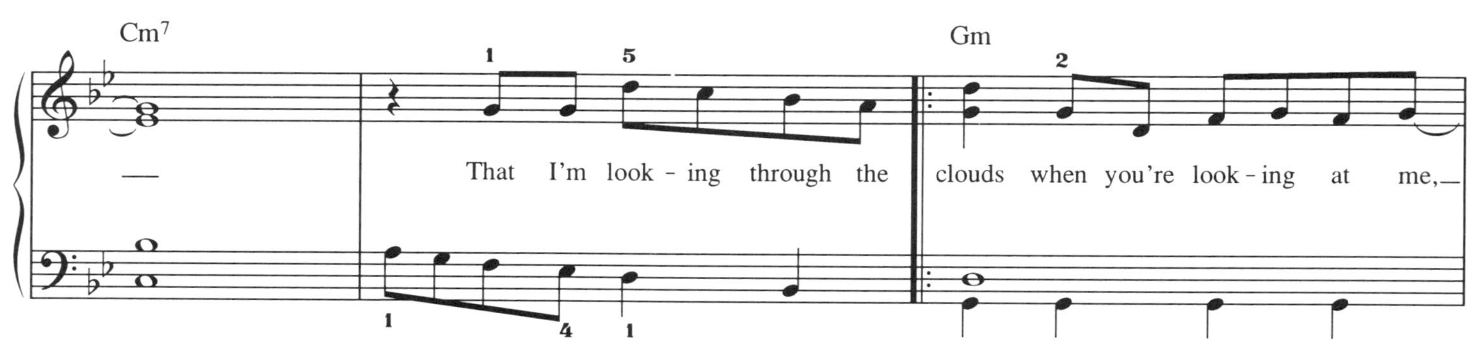
Cm7
1
5
Gm
2
That I'm look - ing through the
clouds when you're look - ing at me,
1
4
1

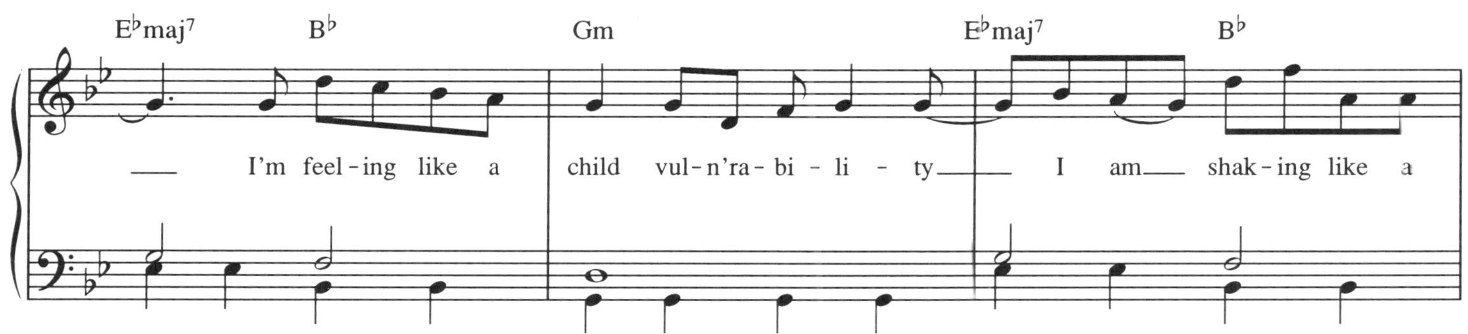

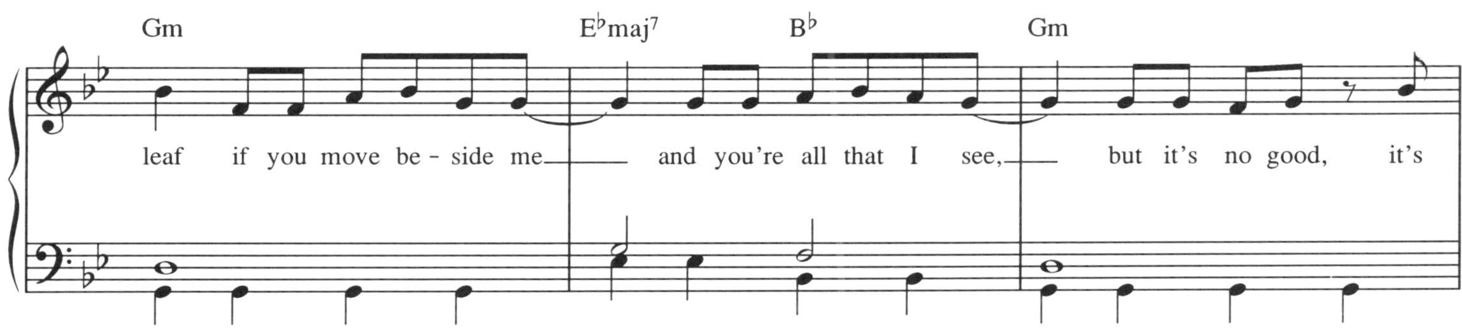

Verse 2:

You have a home in a quiet place
And someone else feels your strong embrace
She is protected and she needs no chase
And do you love her?

You're a mystery,
You are the heart of intrigue,
You're no good no, no good for me
That you have no idea.

That I'm walking through the clouds *etc.*

Only When I Sleep

Words & Music by Andrea Corr, Caroline Corr, Sharon Corr,
Jim Corr, John Shanks, Paul Peterson & Oliver Leiber

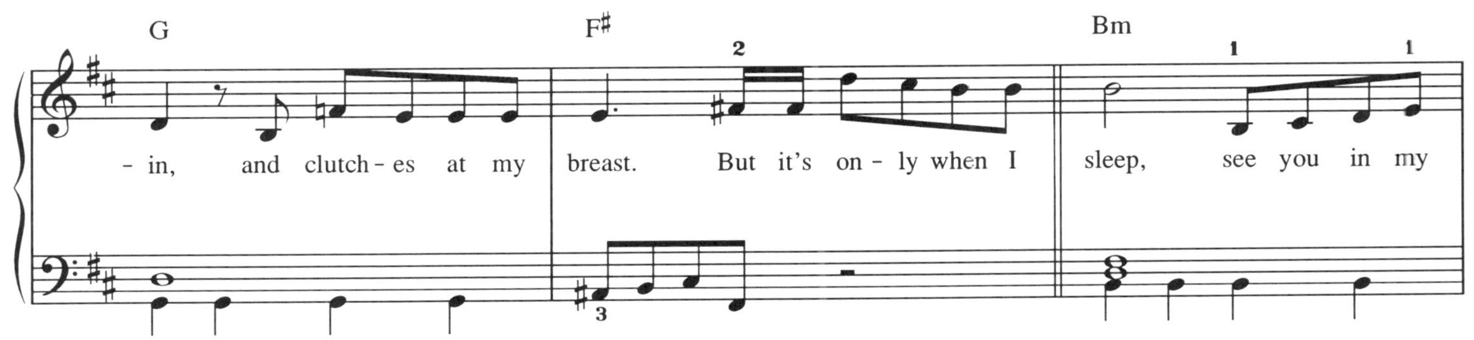
G
F♯
Bm
2
1
1
- in, and clutch - es at my
breast. But it's on - ly when I
sleep, see you in my
3

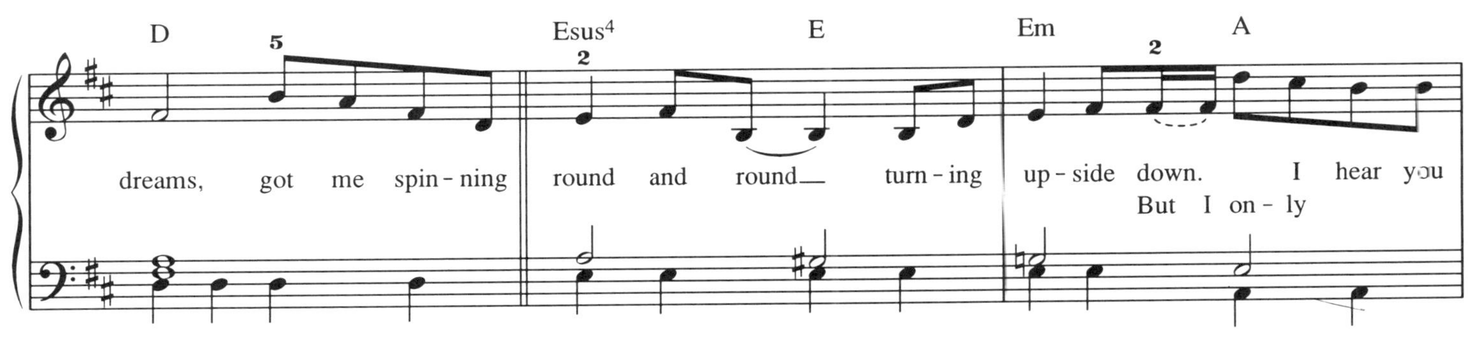
D
Esus4
E
Em
A
5
2
2
dreams, got me spin - ning
round and round turn - ing
up - side down. I hear you
But I on - ly

Bm
D
Esus4
E
breathe some - where in my
dreams, got me spin - ning
round and round turn - ing

Em
A
G
E
D
A
1
3
up - side down, on - ly when I sleep.
Yeah
Yeah
Yeah
5

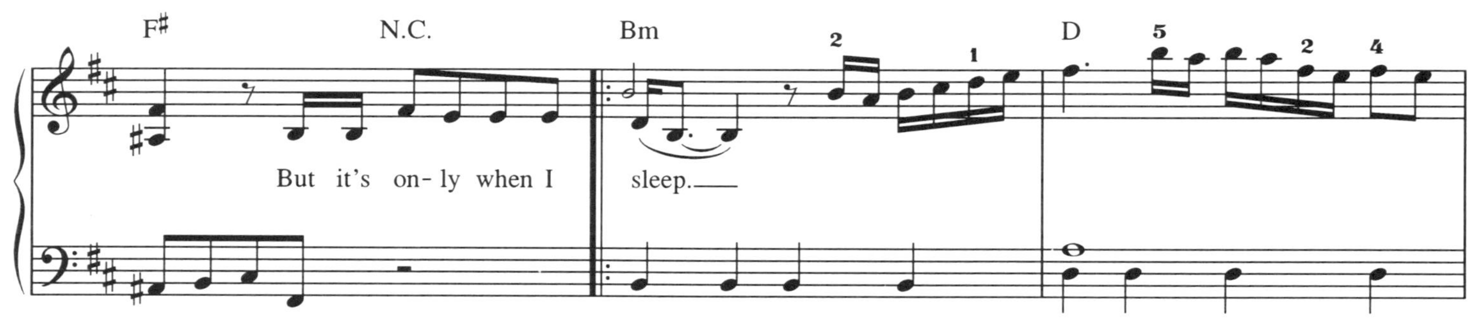
F♯
N.C.
Bm
D
But it's on- ly when I
sleep.

Esus4
E
Em
A
G
It's reach - ing through my

D
G
F♯
skin, mo - ving from with - in, it clutch - es at my breast yeah.

Bm
D
But it's on- ly when I sleep, See you in my dreams, got me spin - ning

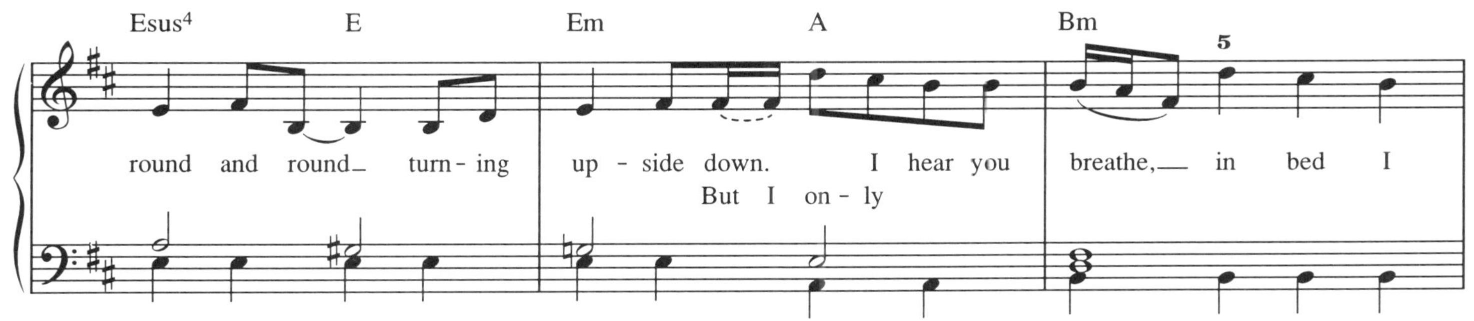

Verse 2:

And when I wake from slumber
Your shadow's disappeared
Your breath is just a sea mist
Surrounding my body
I'm working through the daytime
But when it's time to rest
I'm lying in my bed
Listening to my breath
Falling from the edge
But I only hear you breathe ....

Runaway

Words & Music by Andrea Corr, Caroline Corr, Sharon Corr & Jim Corr

Dm
B♭
run a - way,
I would have
Gm7
C7
run a - way,
yeah,
yeah.
I would have
Dm
B♭
run a - way,
I would have
Gm7
C
run a - way
with
you.
'Cause
F
Gm7
B♭
I
have
fall - en in

F
Gm7
B♭
love
with
F
Gm7
B♭
you. No,
ne - ver,
I'm
ne - ver gon - na
F
Gm7
C
B♭
C7
To Coda
stop
fall - ing in
love
with
1.
F
Gm7
F
you.
2
1
3
2.
F
Gm7
B♭/C
you,
with
1
4
3

F
you.

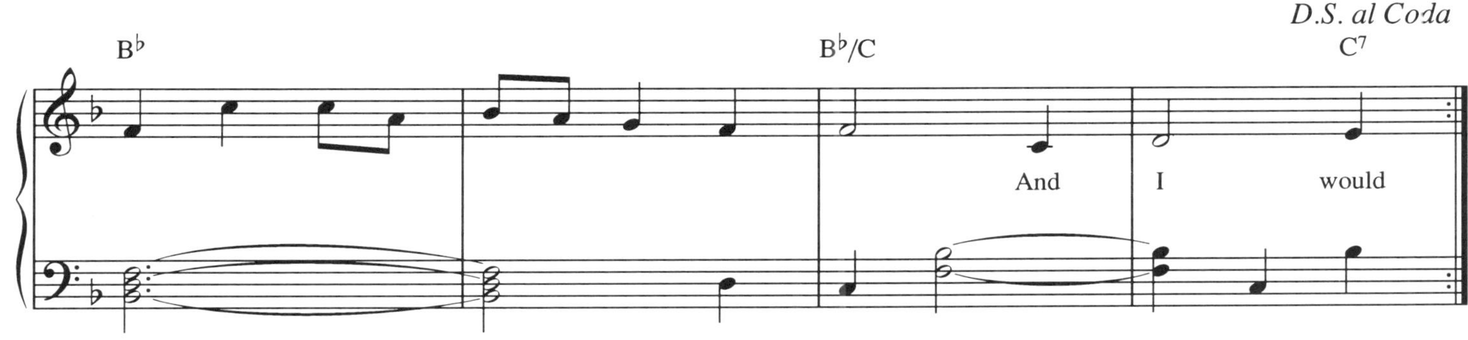
D.S. al Coda
B♭
B♭/C
C7
And
I
would

CODA
F
Gm7
C7
you,
with

F
Gm7
F
you.

So Young

Words & Music by Andrea Corr, Caroline Corr, Sharon Corr & Jim Corr

Am
C
D
And it real - ly does - n't mat - ter that we don't eat, and it
Am
C
D
Am
real - ly does - n't mat - ter that we ne - ver sleep, and it real - ly does - n't mat - ter, real -
C
Dsus4
D
- ly does - n't mat - ter at all. 'Cause we are
G
C
D
so young now and we are so young, so young now.
G
C
and when to - mor - row comes we can / we'll just do it all a - gain.

D
1.
2. And we are
2.
Yeah we are
G
C
D
so young now, we are so young, so young now.
and when to - mor - row comes we'll just do it all a - gain,
To Coda
D
Am
all a - gain,
C
Em
D
all a - gain,
all a - gain,

Verse 2:

We are chasing the moon
Just running wild and free,
We are following through
Every dream and every need.

'Cause we are so young now *etc.*

What Can I Do

Words & Music by Andrea Corr, Caroline Corr, Sharon Corr & Jim Corr

C
G
F
What can I do to make you love me?
C
G
Dm
What can I do to make you care?
C
G
F
What can I do to make you feel this?
C
G
Dm
To Coda
What can I do to get you there?
Am7
C
G
F
G
No more wait - ing, no more ach - ing

D.C. al Coda
Am7
C
G
F
G
No more fight - ing, no more try - ing
CODA
C
3
G
F
What can I do to make you love me?
C
G
Dm
What can I say to make you care?
C
G
F
What can I say to make you feel this?
C
G
Dm
What can I do to get you there and love me?

Verse 2:

There's only so much I can take
And I just got to let it go
And who knows I might feel better
If I don't try and I don't hope.

What can I do...

Queen Of Hollywood

Words & Music by Andrea Corr, Caroline Corr, Sharon Corr,
Jim Corr, Glenn Ballard, Dane de Viller & Sean Hosein

Dsus4
C
Am7
D
Em7
there. She's ne - ver gon - na be like the one be - fore,
she read it in her
C
Am7
D
C
Am7
stars that there's some - thing more,
no mat - ter what it takes no mat - ter how she
D
Em7
C
breaks, she'll be the queen of Hol - ly - wood.
3,4.
C
Dsus4
C
Am7
scene, and a shi - ning li - mou - sine. She's ne - ver gon - na be like the one be - fore,
D
Em
C
Am7
D
she read it in her stars that there's some - thing more,
no mat - ter what it

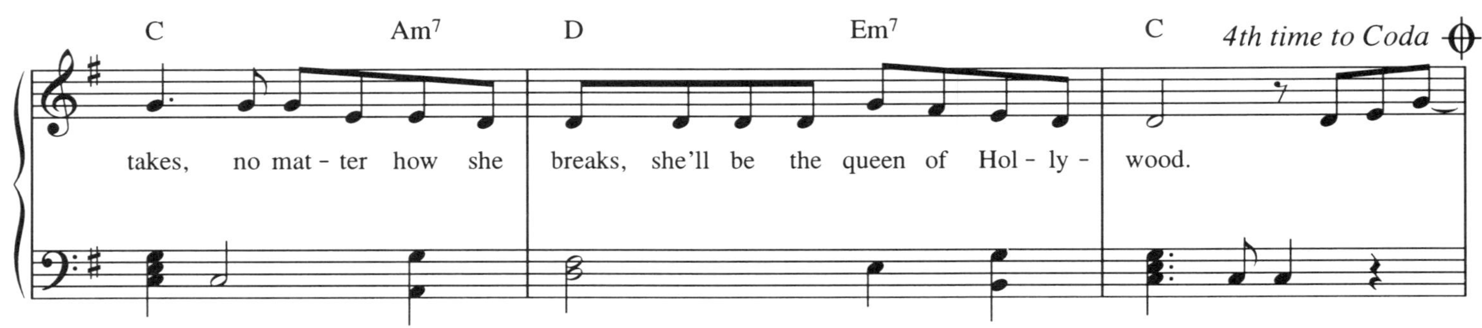
C
Am7
D
Em7
C
4th time to Coda
takes, no mat - ter how she breaks, she'll be the queen of Hol - ly - wood.

G/B
F
C
she's be - liev - ing in a dream,

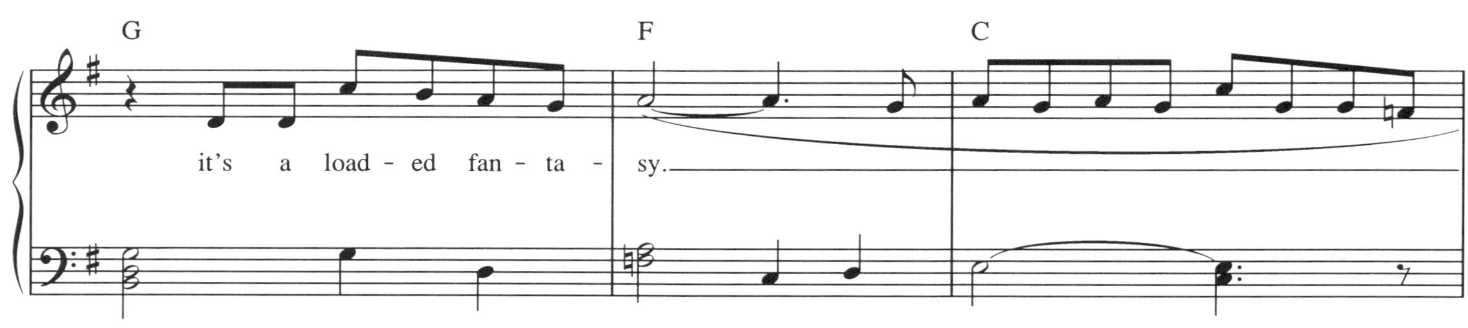
G
F
C
it's a load - ed fan - ta - sy.

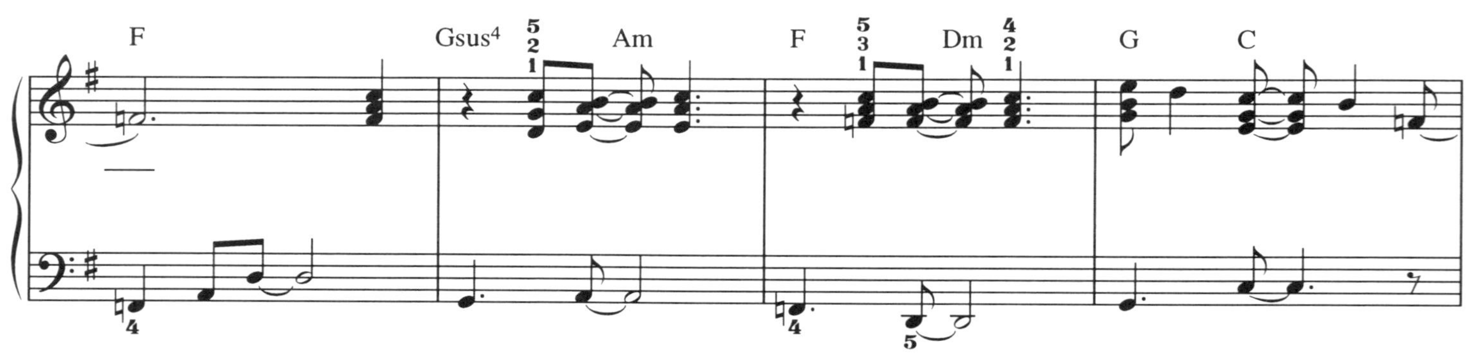
F
Gsus4
Am
F
Dm
G
C

D.C. al Coda
F
Dm7
Gsus4
Am
F
Fadd9

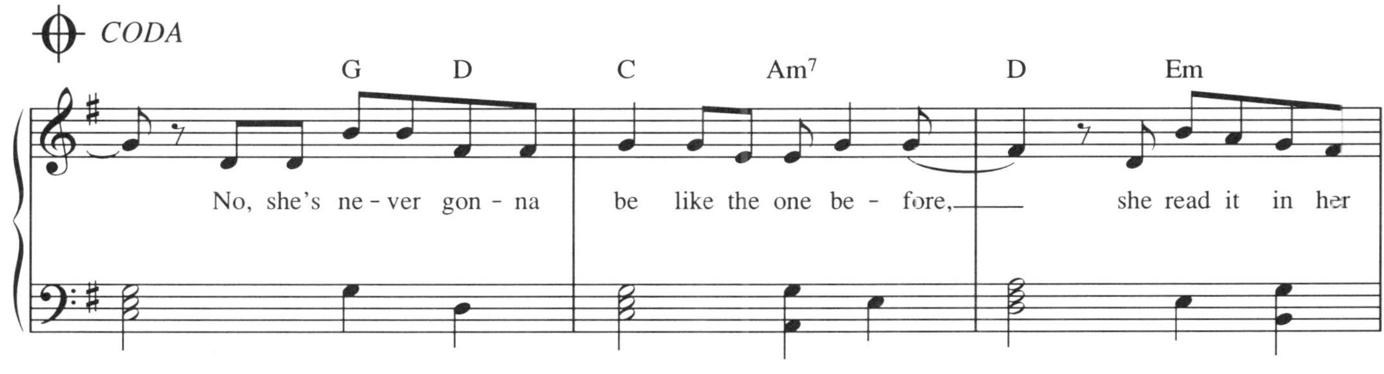
CODA
G
D
C
Am7
D
Em
No, she's ne - ver gon - na
be like the one be - fore,
she read it in her

C
Am7
D
C
Am7
stars that there's some - thing more,
no mat - ter what it
takes, and ev - en though she

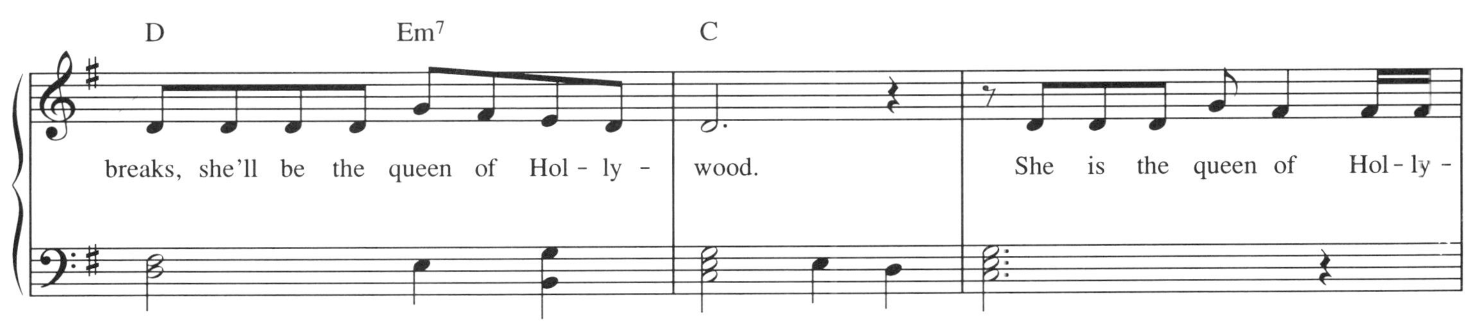
D
Em7
C
breaks, she'll be the queen of Hol - ly -
wood.
She is the queen of Hol - ly -

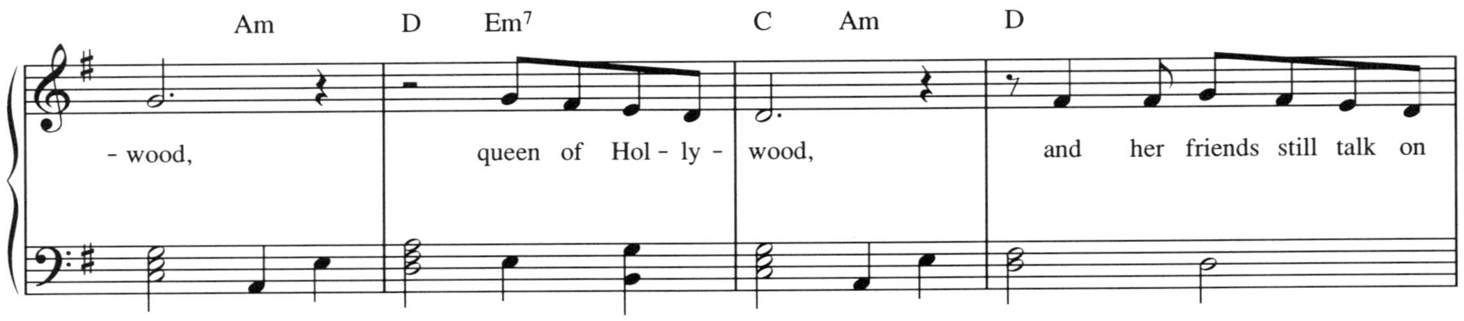

Verse 2:
But there was always something different
In the way she held a stare
And the pictures that she painted
Were of glamour and of flair.
And her boyfriend though he loved her
Knew he couldn't quite fulfil
He could never meet her there.

Verse 3:
And the cynics they will wonder
What's the difference with this dream
And the dreams of countless others
All believing in T.V.
They see their handprints in a sidewalk
Flashing cameras on the scene
And a shining limousine.

Verse 4:
Now her mother collects cut-outs
And the pictures make her smile
But if she saw behind the curtains
It could only make her cry.
She's got handprints on her body
Sad moonbeams in her eyes
Not so innocent a child.

9/00 (38157)